LEAPING LEMURS, TUMBLING TOADS, JET-PROPELLED JELLYFISH, AND MORE SURPRISING WAYS THAT ANIMALS MOVE

FLYING FROGS
AND
WALKING FISH

BY STEVE JENKINS AND ROBIN PAGE

HOUGHTON MIFFLIN HARCOURT   BOSTON   NEW YORK

A nimals walk, leap, climb, and swim. Some roll or turn flips. Others fly or glide, and a few are even jet-propelled. These creatures are found in many shapes and sizes. They come equipped with legs, fins, wings, or tentacles, and they often get from place to place in surprising ways. Have you ever seen . . .

A Walking Octopus?

Yes! A **common octopus** has eight legs, but it often uses just two of them to walk on the sea floor.

For many animals, walking is the simplest way to get around. It doesn't take a lot of energy, and the slow pace makes it easy to watch for food or danger. Some animals walk in unusual ways, and others choose unexpected places to walk.

Marching, strolling, tiptoeing . . .

A **fishing spider** stays high and dry as it walks on the water's surface.

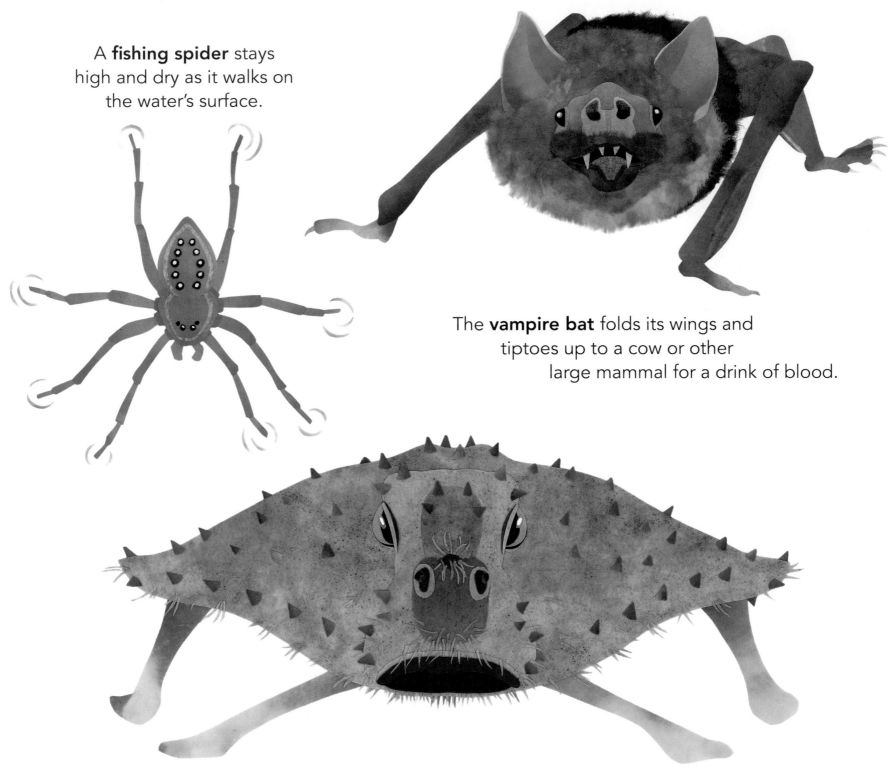

The **vampire bat** folds its wings and tiptoes up to a cow or other large mammal for a drink of blood.

A **red-lipped batfish** waddles across the sea floor on its fins, searching for small sea creatures to eat.

Deep in the ocean, a **sea pig** strolls along on its tubelike feet.

As it walks, a **red kangaroo** uses its tail as a fifth leg.

A **millipede** marches along by getting its legs—as many as 750 of them—to work together.

A Leaping Lizard?

An **agama** fits the bill. This agile lizard can leap several times its own body length.

Sometimes an animal needs to get to a new spot in a hurry. Maybe a predator is chasing it. Perhaps it *is* a predator, and it's leaping to grab its prey. It could be sending a message, or simply trying to get a better look around.

Jumping, pouncing, springing . . .

Ready, aim, pounce! A **jumping spider** can leap fifty times its own body length.

An **Adélie penguin** rockets from the water and lands—plop!—on an ice floe.

A **springbok** bounds straight up. This tells predators, "I won't be easy to catch."

High above the ground, a **ring-tailed lemur** vaults from tree to tree.

A **manta ray** bursts from the water, then lands with a terrific splash.

To impress its mate, a **Japanese red-crowned crane** springs into the air and flutters back to earth.

A Swimming Elephant?

Despite its bulk, the **Indian elephant** is a strong swimmer. By using its trunk as a snorkel, it can breathe when its mouth is underwater.

Rivers, lakes, and oceans can be challenging environments for animals adapted to life on land or in the air. But swimming, even awkwardly, helps many creatures cool off, find food, or escape danger.

Cruising, paddling, diving . . .

A young **baboon** dives in and paddles around just for fun.

The **sea butterfly** is a kind of snail. It uses its foot, which is shaped like a pair of wings, to cruise through the water.

It may be slow and awkward on land, but a **three-toed sloth** is right at home in the water.

The **marine iguana** swims beneath the waves to graze on seaweed.

A sleek **cormorant** plunges deep into the sea as it pursues a school of fish.

A Tree-Climbing Goat?

With its soft, grippy hooves and excellent balance, a
domestic goat scampers into the branches of a tree.

Why climb a tree? Sometimes that's where a meal can be found. At other times, the branches of a tree are a safe place where many predators can't follow.

Scrambling, scurrying, slithering . . .

A **hoatzin** (hoh-at-sin) chick can't fly. But it has an extra set of claws on its wings, and it uses them to scurry up a tree if danger threatens.

As it looks for eggs or baby birds to eat, a **black rat snake** slithers up the trunk of a tree.

A **mudskipper** drags itself up the roots of a mangrove tree. There it will be safe from hungry fish in the water below.

A **rat terrier** will sometimes chase a squirrel right up into the branches of a tree.

A **coconut crab** shimmies up a palm tree and snips the stalk of a coconut. Then it clambers down and cracks open its prize with powerful claws.

A Flying Snake?

A **flying snake** can't fly like an eagle or a butterfly, but it can glide through the air. It drops from a branch, flattens its body, and sails to a nearby tree.

Some animals are true fliers. They flap their wings and can stay airborne for long periods of time. Others are gliders—they sail through the air, but for only a limited distance. Both fliers and gliders often take to the air to escape danger.

Gliding, soaring, coasting . . .

As it coasts from tree to tree, a **sugar glider** steers itself with its tail.

Gliding ants nest high in the treetops. If an ant falls off, it uses its flattened head and legs to drift, rear end first, back to its home tree.

A **Draco lizard** avoids predators by unfurling folds of skin and gliding to safety.

The **flying frog** launches itself into space, spreads its webbed fingers and toes, and glides away.

A **rhinoceros beetle** is capable of true flight— a surprising ability for such a large and bulky insect.

Once it leaves the water, a **flying fish** can soar the length of a football field on its outstretched fins.

A Rolling Spider?

A **Moroccan desert spider** "flic-flacs"—turns flips across the sand dunes—to escape predators.

For most animals, turning end over end is not an efficient way to get around. But for some creatures, being able to roll or cartwheel away from danger can mean the difference between life and death.

Whirling, tumbling, somersaulting . . .

If it gets stranded on the beach, a **mantis shrimp** somersaults back to the water.

A frightened **pebble toad** pushes off from its rocky mountainside perch and tumbles downhill like a dislodged pebble.

A **hedgehog** turns into a curled-up pincushion and makes its escape by rolling away.

A **tiger beetle larva** curls up and lets the wind whirl it along the ground.

An **armadillo lizard** bites its tail to form a spiny circle. On sloping ground, it can wheel away from danger.

A **pangolin** rolls into an armored ball to defend itself. If the terrain allows, it will roll away from a threat.

A Jet-Propelled Fish?

A **frogfish** hovers above the sea floor and surges forward by expelling water from its gills.

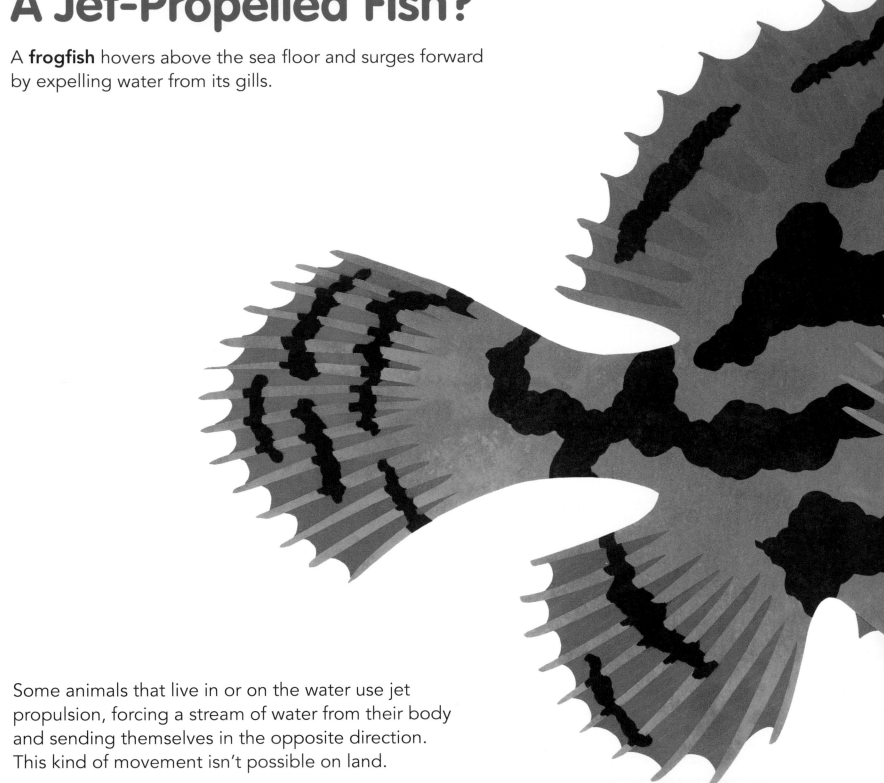

Some animals that live in or on the water use jet propulsion, forcing a stream of water from their body and sending themselves in the opposite direction. This kind of movement isn't possible on land.

Pulsing, jetting, zooming . . .

A **vampire squid** glides backwards by forcing water from its siphon, a tube on its body.

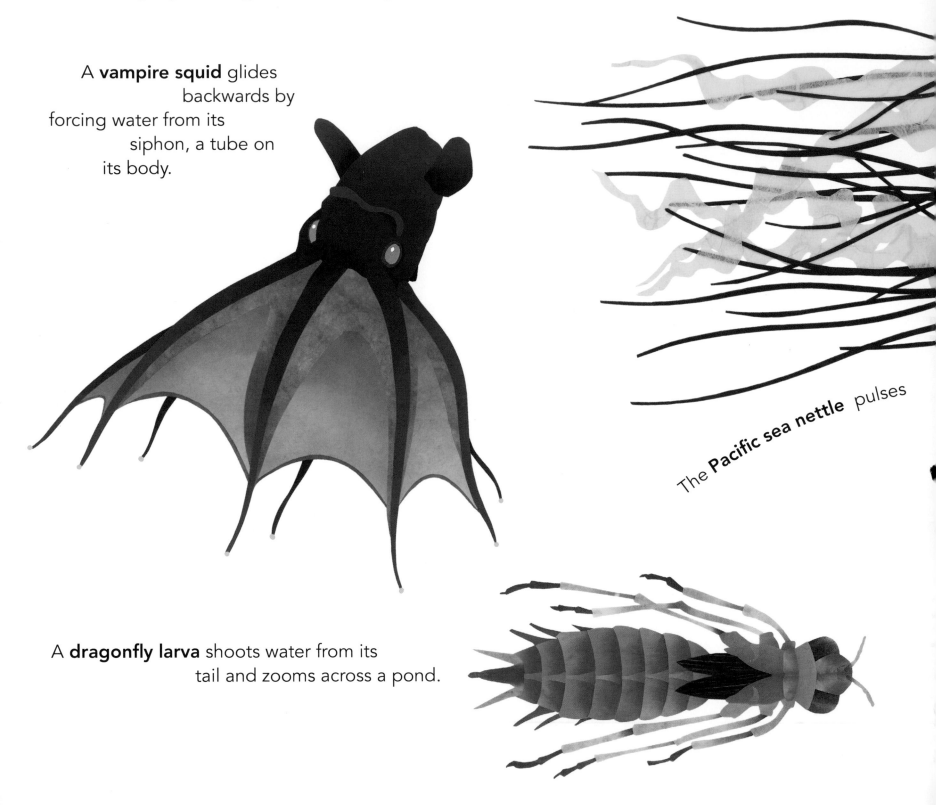

The **Pacific sea nettle** pulses

A **dragonfly larva** shoots water from its tail and zooms across a pond.

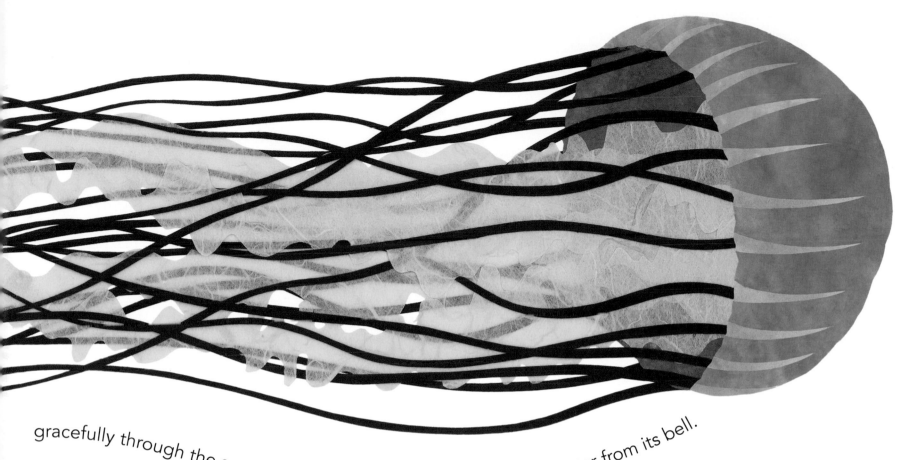

gracefully through the sea by contracting its body and pushing water from its bell.

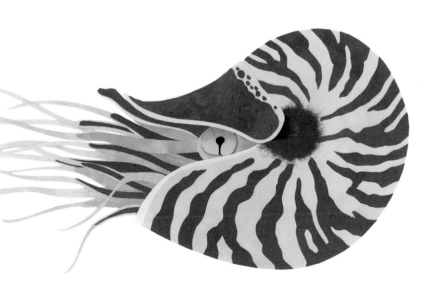

The **nautilus** expels water from its shell and propels itself through the sea.

By clamping its two shells together, a **scallop** squirts out water and jets to safety.

Walking

The **common octopus** lives in warm coastal waters worldwide. It grows to 36 inches (91 centimeters) in length and feeds on fish, crabs, and shellfish.

The **vampire bat** lives in Central and South America. It sleeps during the day, emerging at night to search for blood, its only food. It has a wingspan of about seven inches (18 centimeters). A vampire bat walks quietly up to its victim — perhaps a sleeping cow, deer, or human. It makes a painless cut with its razor-sharp teeth, then laps up the blood as it oozes out.

The fishing spider in this book is a **six-spotted fishing spider,** named for the six dark spots on its belly. It lives near fresh water throughout much of North America. Including its legs, it can reach two and a half inches (5 centimeters) in length, and it hunts insects and small fish.

The **red-lipped batfish** lives on the sea floor of the Pacific Ocean near the Galápagos Islands. It grows to ten inches (25 centimeters) in length. Batfish eat fish, shrimp, and crabs.

The **sea pig,** a kind of sea cucumber, is about six inches (15 centimeters) long. It lives on the sea floor in deep parts of the world's oceans and feeds on tiny organic particles in the mud.

A **red kangaroo** can stand five feet (1½ meters) tall and weigh 200 pounds (91 kilograms). It inhabits the deserts and grasslands of Australia. Kangaroos cannot move their back legs independently, so they either hop on two legs or walk using four legs and their tail.

Most **millipedes** have about 100 legs, but the millipede in this book — its Latin name means "the acme of plentiful legs" — has as many as 750. It is only about one inch (2½ centimeters) long. It has been found in just one small area in Northern California, where it feeds on plant juices.

Leaping

During its breeding season, the male **agama** lizard, normally a dull brown, becomes brightly colored to attract females. Agamas live in arid parts of western Africa and feed on insects. They grow to about 12 inches (30 centimeters) in length.

Standing just over two feet (61 centimeters) tall, the **Adélie penguin** lives in the coastal regions of Antarctica, where it hunts squid, fish, and krill. These penguins form colonies that can include hundreds of thousands of birds.

There are thousands of species of **jumping spider,** with bodies ranging in size from ⅟₂₅ inch to one inch (1–25 millimeters) long. Rather than building webs, most jumping spiders stalk and attack insects and other spiders. They are found almost everywhere on earth.

The **springbok** grazes on grasses and shrubs on the plains of southern Africa. This antelope stands less than three feet (91 centimeters) tall, but it can leap six and a half feet (2 meters) straight up into the air, a behavior known as "pronking."

The **ring-tailed lemur** lives in the forests of Madagascar. It is an herbivore, feeding on fruit, flowers, leaves, and bark. Like all lemurs, it is at home in the treetops. It is about 18 inches (46 centimeters) long, not counting its tail.

The **manta ray** is the largest of the rays, with a wingspan of up to 23 feet (7 meters). Manta rays live in temperate and tropical ocean waters worldwide and eat plankton — small plants and animals that drift through the water — as they swim. Despite the manta ray's size, it is gentle and harmless to humans.

The **Japanese red-crowned crane** nests in Siberia, northeastern China, and northern Japan. This elegant bird stands five feet (1½ meters) tall and feeds on fish, amphibians, insects, and water plants.

Swimming

The **Indian elephant** may be smaller than its African cousin, but it can still stand more than ten feet tall and weigh as much as 11,000 pounds (5,000 kilograms). Indian elephants spend most of their time eating. They feed primarily on grass, but will consume fruit, leaves, bark, and roots. They live in the grasslands and forests of India and Southeast Asia.

The **sea butterfly** is an ocean-dwelling snail with a shell about ½ inch (1¼ centimeters) across. Sea butterflies live in all of the world's oceans, and feed on plankton.

A large male **baboon** can weigh as much as 90 pounds (41 kilograms). Baboons live in the forests and savannas of Africa, as well as in some coastal regions of Arabia. They eat fruit, grasses, seeds, bird's eggs, and small animals.

The Galápagos Islands are home to the **marine iguana.** This five-foot (1½ meter)-long lizard feeds on underwater algae. Like all reptiles, it is cold-blooded. After swimming in cold ocean waters, it warms itself by basking in the sun.

The **three-toed sloth** lives in the rain-forests of Central and South America. It spends almost all of its time hanging upside down from the branches of a tree. This slow-moving mammal grows to about 20 inches (51 centimeters) in length and eats leaves and fruit.

The **cormorant** has a wingspan of four feet (1¼ meters) or more. It is common in coastal waters throughout the world, especially in places where cliffs or rocky shorelines provide shelter. Cormorants eat fish and shellfish.

Climbing

Goats are raised all over the world for their milk, meat, and wool. There are many different breeds of **domestic goat.** The smallest stands just 18 inches (46 centimeters) tall, while the largest can weigh as much as 300 pounds (136 kilograms). Goats eat fruit, vegetables, leaves, shrubs, and grasses.

The **hoatzin** has bacteria in its gut that helps it digest the leaves it eats. This digestive system has earned it the nickname "stinkbird." Hoatzins are about 24 inches (61 centimeters) long and live in the Amazonian rainforest. As adults, the birds lose the claws on their wings. They are poor fliers and spend most of their time perched in trees.

The **mudskipper** can breathe with gills or through its skin, so it spends time both in and out of the water. It is found in the coastal swamps and mudflats of East Africa, Southeast Asia, and Australia. Mudskippers grow to ten inches (25 centimeters) in length and eat insects and small animals.

The **black rat snake** reaches eight feet (2½ meters) in length. It inhabits the woodlands of the eastern United States, where it preys on birds, rodents, and other small animals. Black rat snakes are constrictors – they squeeze their prey to death before consuming it.

The **rat terrier** was bred as a farm and hunting dog, and was often kept to control rats and other vermin. Today, the breed is more common as a family pet. These intelligent and energetic dogs average 20 pounds (9 kilograms) in weight.

Including its legs, the **coconut crab** grows to more than three feet (91 centimeters) in length. This huge crab lives in burrows on the coasts of the Pacific and Indian Oceans. In addition to coconuts, it eats fruit, small animals, and carrion (dead animals).

Flying

The **flying snake** spends its life in the trees of India and Southeast Asia. It can reach lengths of four feet (1¼ meters) and hunts birds, rodents, frogs, and other small animals.

The **sugar glider** weighs only four or five ounces (113–142 grams). It is a marsupial—females nurture their babies in a pouch. Sugar gliders feed on insects, tree sap, and small animals. They live in trees in eastern and northern Australia and on some islands in the South Pacific.

Gliding ants live in the rainforests of Central and South America. They nest in the treetops and feed on plant pollen, bird droppings, and other insects. Worker ants are about one half-inch (1¼ centimeters) long. If a gliding ant falls or is knocked from its perch, it steers itself back to its tree. If it bounces off, it can make a U-turn in the air and try again.

The **Draco lizard** lives in the jungles of Southeast Asia. It is about eight inches (20 centimeters) long. It spends most of its time in the trees, feeding on ants and termites and gliding to safety if danger threatens.

There are many species of frogs that have the ability to glide through the air. The frog in this book is a **Wallace's flying frog.** It is about four inches (10 centimeters) long, and makes its home in the rain forests of New Guinea, Malaysia, and Borneo. These frogs eat insects, and spend most of their lives in the trees.

Rhinoceros beetles are found on every continent except Antarctica. The beetle in this book is a **five-horned rhinoceros beetle.** It lives in Southeast Asia and is about three inches (7½ centimeters) long. Rhinoceros beetles feed on fruit, sap, and nectar.

Flying fish inhabit tropical and subtropical ocean waters around the world. These fish can reach 18 inches (46 centimeters) in length. They feed on plankton and small marine animals.

Rolling

The **Moroccan desert spider** lives in the deserts of northwestern Africa. It was unknown to science until 2014. This spider spends the day in a burrow beneath the sand, emerging at night to hunt for insects. Its body is about three-fourths of an inch (19 millimeters) long.

The **mantis shrimp** inhabits warm-water coral reefs around the world. It grows to 12 inches (30 centimeters) in length. Mantis shrimp use a modified claw to pierce or bludgeon the shellfish, shrimp, and crabs they prey on.

The **pebble toad** lives in the mountains of Venezuela, where it feeds on worms and insects. It is less than one inch (2½ centimeters) long – so small that it is not hurt when it bounces down a rocky mountainside.

The **hedgehog** is found throughout much of Europe, Asia, and Africa. It grows to about eight inches (20 centimeters) in length and eats insects, worms, frogs, and other small animals.

The adult tiger beetle is a fierce, fast-running predator. The **tiger beetle larva** is equally fierce. It lurks in a burrow, and when an insect or spider comes near, the larva seizes its victim and pulls it underground. These beetles are common in temperate and tropical regions worldwide. The larvae are about one inch (2½ centimeters) long.

The **armadillo lizard** lives along the western coast of South Africa. Its body is about three and a half inches (9 centimeters) long. It eats insects and spiders, and occasionally feeds on plants.

The **pangolin** is a kind of armored anteater. The tough scales that cover its body are made of keratin – the same material as our fingernails. Pangolins live in warm parts of Asia and in Africa south of the Sahara Desert. They can reach 39 inches (1 meter) in length, and use their long, sticky tongue to capture ants and termites.

Jetting

Frogfish are found in the warm waters of Atlantic, Pacific, and Indian Oceans. The fish in this book, the **sargassum frogfish,** lives in areas where there is an accumulation of seaweed. It is about eight inches (20 centimeters) long. Frogfish are predators. They capture their prey—mostly fish and shrimp—by sucking them in and swallowing them whole.

The **vampire squid** looks frightening, but it is only about six inches (15 centimeters) long. It lives in the deep, dark waters of temperate and tropical oceans worldwide. Vampire squid hunt and eat shrimp and other small marine animals.

The **Pacific sea nettle** drifts through the Pacific coastal waters of North America and Japan. Its bell is about 12 inches (30 centimeters) in diameter, and its trailing tentacles can be 15 feet (4½ meters) in length. These jellyfish hunt by trailing their venomous tentacles through the water, stunning and killing plankton, fish, and other jellyfish.

There are thousands of dragonfly species. They are found on every continent except Antarctica. All dragonflies go through a larval stage as part of their life cycle. **Dragonfly larvae** live in the water, and can reach two inches (5 centimeters) in length. They are predators, feeding on insects, tadpoles, and small fish.

The **nautilus** lives in the warm waters of the Indo-Pacific Ocean. The shell of a large nautilus may be ten inches (25 centimeters) across, though most are smaller. These mollusks are scavengers, eating dead sea creatures and small marine animals.

Scallops are found in every ocean in the world. The shell of the largest species can reach eight inches (20 centimeters) in width. Most scallops are free swimmers, using jet propulsion to escape danger. They feed on plankton filtered from the water.

For Rafi

To learn about the making of this book go to
stevejenkinsbooks.com/flyingfrogs

Bibliography

The Animal Book. By Steve Jenkins. Houghton Mifflin Harcourt, 2013.

Animal Fact File. By Dr. Tony Hare. Checkmark Books, 1999.

Animal Life. By Jill Bailey. Oxford University Press, 1994.

The Encyclopedia of Mammals. Edited by David Macdonald. The Brown Reference Group, 2001.

How Animals Work. By David Burnie. Dorling Kindersley, 2010.

Move! By Steve Jenkins and Robin Page. Houghton Mifflin Harcourt, 2006.

Unusual Creatures. By Michael Hearst. Chronicle Books, 2012.

The Usborne Book of Animal Facts. By Anita Ganeri. Usborne Publishing, 1988.

Wildlife Factfinder. By Martin Walters. Dempsey Parr, 1999.

The text of this book is set in Avenir.

The illustrations are torn- and cut-paper collage.

Library of Congress Cataloging-in-Publication Data

Jenkins, Steve, 1952–author.

Flying frogs and walking fish : leaping lemurs, tumbling toads, jet-propelled jellyfish, and more surprising ways that animals move / by Steve Jenkins and Robin Page.

     pages cm

Audience: Ages 4–8.

Audience: K to grade 3.

Includes bibliographical references.

ISBN 978-0-544-63090-1

1. Animal locomotion – Juvenile literature. 2. Marine animals – Locomotion – Juvenile literature. I. Page, Robin, 1957– author. II. Title.

QP301.J436 2015
591.5'7 – dc23
2015011620

www.hmhco.com

ISBN: 978-0-544-63090-1

Manufactured in China
SCP 10 9 8 7 6 5 4 3 2 1
4500575249

DISCARD